I0069304

Networking
is NOT
a One-night Stand

*A Guide for Building Lasting
Business Relationships*

Tish Times

Copyright © 2016 Tish Times

All rights reserved.

ISBN-10: 0692760458

ISBN-13: 978-0692760451 (Tish Times Enterprises)

FOREWORD

Networking. The very word makes many shudder. Attending an event where you know no one, then approaching a perfect stranger, and engaging in a conversation, to see what you can get from them? Yes. That would make me shudder, too. I remember when I started networking; I HATED IT!!!

I hated it so badly that I invested six thousand dollars in a training program that taught me how to network effectively. Was it worth it? Absolutely! However, Networking is Not a One-night Stand gives you the principles of what I learned in that training class for a fraction of the price.

As a result of learning to network the right way, my business has grown globally. In fact, all of my success in life and business can circle back to networking.

Although networking is about building long-

DEDICATION

Roy Times—my husband who is my BFF and lifelong love.

Derrell, Lavell, and Charles—my amazing sons who are a constant inspiration.

Cassandra Pelham (Denise), Rodney Peoples, L.T. Peoples—my siblings who always believe in me.

Dr. Mikel Brown—by whom I was inspired to take the leap into business.

Darnyelle Jervey—my business coach who has encouraged and inspired me in business.

Mary LizzFox Campbell, Latascha Durden, Belinda Johnson, and Caryn Newman— My besties, accountability partners, and prayer warriors.

Gena Davis, Lisa Ann Landry, Tarsha Polk, Star Babatoon, Toni Harris Taylor, Nikki Woods, and Dr. Angela Massey—my business masterminds.

The many other business colleagues and friends who have been in my corner

Thank you!

term business relationships, it is very much like dating. Just like in life, many business relationships fail because we don't know how to nurture them and keep the fire burning as Tish points out in this book. Personal relationships do not happen instantly, so why do we treat our business relationships like they should move from introduction to transaction within minutes? Networking is not about getting a quickie as stated in Chapter 1, but it is about expanding relationships, as we learn in Chapter 8.

I reflect back on how I met Tish while attending a conference in Dallas in August 2013. We connected and promised to stay in touch. Unfortunately, life got busy for both of us, and we did not stay in touch. Here's what I have learned in my networking across the United States and Canada: when connections are meant to be, they show up again. Fast forward to 2015, I'm in a mastermind with seven other dynamic women, and we decide to open up the membership to three more people. One of the Sistars mentions Tish Times. Instantly, I knew who she was, after all who can forget that name? I said, "Yes, we've got to have her in our group!" and the rest as they say, is history.

Tish Times is the ultimate people connector. She is passionate about giving her audience the confidence to be unstoppable in their networking and ultimately their sales. What I love about Tish is her ability to be honest and forthcoming and being able to share her experiences and tell the truth about her journey. In this book, she does just that.

Networking can provide you with the connections that make a difference in your life. Trust the process, it works. It doesn't happen overnight, but when you apply the principles in Networking is Not a One-night Stand, your life can change for the better. Do the work, and the work will pay off! Happy networking!

Toni Harris, "The Turnaround Queen®"

author of Soar2Success in Sales and Marketing

– 78 Tips for

D.R.A.S.T.I.C. Results

PREFACE

When people looked at me in all of my eighteen-year-old glory, often they incorrectly made the assumption that I was this super confident person. It was my own fault. I was five feet eleven. I walked tall with great posture. I smiled all the time. AND, I stood out, being one of the tallest of the few black girls in my high school. I loved the attention; I was the captain of the varsity basketball team on which I played all four years in high school. And I didn't just play ball; I was a baller! I went from having my name announced on the loud speaker after being a high point scorer in the previous night's game to being recognized for being an honor roll student and being the only cheerleader who was allowed to play ball and cheer. I was often the center of attention, and I lived for it.

There was one area of my life where I longed for attention but lacked it: my love life. I was surrounded by friends who already had their first boyfriends, some who were going "steady," and they were all being asked to prom or homecoming. None of that was happening for me. I didn't think I was very pretty, and the lack of attention was confirming that in my mind. All of the confidence that others had created on my behalf was insufficient in helping me feel better about myself in my own head.

Then entered a guy. He was six feet three and a baller in his own right. He would look at me during games, sometimes tell me what a great player I was; then, he asked me out. I swooned when he first touched my hand, and, OMG, that first kiss! Wow! Is this what everyone has been talking about? Although I thought he was "all that," I took it very slow.

When I graduated from high school, it started. The silence. No more high fives in the hallway after a game. No more announcements over the loud speaker. No more newspaper highlights. It was just me, and I was not enough.

Then, I started to hang out more with "the guy." He became my cheering squad: "You're so pretty. I love you. You're amazing!" That was all I needed to hear. He filled the silence.

"Of course I'll date you," I cried on the inside. "Of course I'll marry you. I'll do whatever it takes to fill the silence."

It was great. It was fabulous to have someone to hold hands with, to introduce as my boyfriend and then my fiancé and then my husband. Until I couldn't breathe. It was all good until the first time he had his hands around my throat.

Until I understood that he didn't love me at all. Until I was sure that he was going to kill me. It was then, once I had my oldest baby, that I realized I had to go. If not for me, then for Derrell, my son. In that period, I found strength for a lot of things. I was no longer happy allowing someone else to be my confidence. I had a choice to take one of two roads: stay and risk my life or take the risk of escaping and getting caught. I realized that I had to love myself and my son enough to live and to thrive.

I had to learn to fill the silence on my own, to tell myself the things that I needed to hear. Things like I am beautiful, I am enough, I am smart, I am lovable. Then I had to learn to embrace the silence and to know that I am amazing, even when no one is telling me. I used prayer, worship, Bible study, personal development, internal conversations (affirmations/I AM Statements), and coaching to cure the insecurity that would have destroyed my ability to build relationships, to build a business, and even to save my life (oh yeah, I contemplated suicide as well).

Most importantly, as Zig Ziglar said, "Timid salespeople have skinny kids." I thought that was hilarious when I first saw it; however, I then that those skinny kids often grow up to be timid adults because of the example set before them.

I decided that I wanted to be an example for my sons to become strong, confident, empowered young men who can do ANYTHING their hearts desires. All of my sons have grown up to be just that.

Because of this commitment to my children I have dedicated my life to worship and scripture to transform my thinking as well as personal development. Now stands before you today an unstoppable, confident woman, although I didn't start that way This is evidence that you can also build the confidence needed to sell, network, and grow your business with unstoppable confidence and not in fear and desperation. II is that fear and desperation that drives timid salespeople to treat networking like a one-night stand, trying to get as much as they can, as early as they can, before their prospective clients figure out that they don't have what it takes to build a solid relationship that lasts. No more of that. You can build relationships, you can sell and network with confidence, and you can see the results of your confidence in your bottom line. Just keep reading.

CHAPTER ONE

"They may forget what you said, but they will never forget how you made them feel." — Maya Angeleou

STOP ASKING YOUR CLIENTS
FOR QUICKIES

Consider this: You walk into a networking event with the intent of making a few important business connections. You are approached by a person who happens to be on your list of "people to meet during the event." The conversation is going well; you are asking great questions, which leads to you gaining details about the needs of this potential client. Suddenly, the conversation takes an abrupt turn. Your ideal client hastily hands you a key to a hotel room and invites you to join him or her this evening to move the relationship along more quickly. You are flabbergasted! Not only is this NOT the direction you had intended, but the forwardness of this person has made the entire interaction awkward. Once you escape, you find yourself dodging his or her calls, hoping you don't see him or her at other events and just wishing you would have stayed home and washed your hair the night of the initial meeting.

This may seem extreme; however, when we try to move a business relationship along too quickly without nurturing the connection, this is exactly how we make others feel. When we slow down the relationship, we often speed up the success. As sales professionals (by the way, we are ALL sales professionals), we are often influenced by

> When we slow down the relationship, we speed up the success.

the pressure of closing the deal. That's how we pay our bills, right? Well, taking time to sincerely understand the needs of our prospective clients builds trust that can lead to real, lasting business relationships and even friendships. During your next initial business encounter, consider how it would feel to be propositioned. Consider how

offensive that feeling is for you, then slow down your approach with the intent of being the problem solver your new connection needs. Genuine interactions, flawless follow-up, and sincere nurturing will change the way you network and ultimately increase your income.

If you wouldn't marry someone you know nothing about, you shouldn't expect to have a thriving business relationship with a contact with whom you have not invested time in "business dating" to understand his or her needs, goals, and desires. The most important relationships take time to develop. Even if the connection is fast, the friendship is perpetually building, and you are constantly learning about each other.

Consider the best, most successful friendship, or romantic relationship in your life. Even if you immediately hit it off, it still took time to get to know one another and understand what makes the other one tick. If you really think about it, wasn't it worth the time investment?

Contrary to popular belief, the most successful salespeople are not necessarily the "cold callers" or "hard sellers." The great salespeople of the world are not those who rush through an interaction just to get a credit card number or check in hand. The best of the best are those who know how to build relationships. Making an investment in sincere relationships will take you beyond transactional interactions. In most cases, once you develop a relationship with a potential client, you often build the level of trust that leads to long-term loyalty.

CHAPTER TWO

"The way to self-confidence is to do the thing you fear and get a record of successful experiences behind you."
— William Jennings Bryan

CONFIDENCE
FOR RELATIONSHIP BUILDING

The question of the hour: Can confidence really be learned or is it innate? I have done some research, but I don't have a scientific answer. All that I have are case studies of those who I've worked with, as well as the personal transformation that I have experienced. I don't think that only a select few receive the gift of confidence at birth, although there are some who appear to be very confident even as children.

Some people may allow what made them unique as children to contribute to low self-esteem. Characteristics such as being very tall, having a darker skin color than others in my peer group, and having what some say is "nappy hair" in a community not heavily populated with African Americans caused me to see myself as different. I didn't have the consistent reinforcement of hearing things like "you are pretty" or "embrace your height" or "you have so much talent" until much later in life. For many years, I equated "different" to not good enough. Though the story may be different for each one of us, we rarely see the correlation between our lack of confidence in connecting with others and not having self-worth earlier in our lives.

The constant reinforcement of positive words (coupled with other exercises) has an enormous impact on the way we see ourselves. The problem occurs when we wait for outside sources to provide us with the encouragement that we so desperately seek inside. I believe that God left us a blueprint for how to use our own internal dialogue to improve our self-confidence. Scripture says, "body and soul, I am marvelously made!" There you can find this and so many other motivating and exhorting phrases that can be used as reminders that "you are MORE than enough!"

Until we understand who we really are and what we are capable of, networking with confidence may always be a struggle. Lack of confidence can influence behaviors such as overcompensating by droning on and on about ourselves instead of asking questions that would help us to understand what the prospective client needs. Low self-worth may prevent us from serving

> You will only act in accordance with your most dominant belief.

a client who really needs our help, because we are afraid that we will fail or that our product or service isn't good enough. When we present our product or service confidently, we are more attractive to those who we can help with our service or product making us more successful with our networking.

My inability to see myself as a woman with tremendous value caused me to settle for bad relationships. I thought that I had to marry the first man who told me I was pretty. I felt as though I had to wear provocative clothing in order to gain the attention of potential boyfriends. I allowed myself to be moved along faster than I should have, and I moved relationships along too quickly, thinking that if I didn't make men like me early enough I would lose the opportunity to have them in my life.

When sales professionals don't see themselves as high-level experts with the ability to positively impact lives, they act similarly. They talk fast and move quickly, hoping to get contracts signed before they are found out to be frauds. In most cases, they aren't fraudulent characters; however, you will only act according to your most dominant belief.

CHAPTER THREE

*"Perserverence is failing nineteen times
and succeeding the twentieth."*
— Julie Andrews

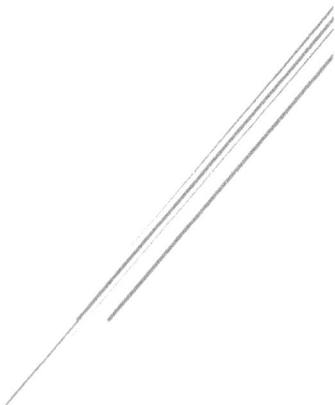

YOU SAID YOU WERE GOING TO CALL!

It's the day after the big conference! You are pumped. You are making calls like a machine, sending out "it was great to meet you" emails. Still high on the content you learned, you're living in the conference afterglow.

It's a week after the conference. You are still working through the stack of business cards you collected. You feel like you've left a million messages. "I thought they were excited to reconnect," you say in your heart. "Why won't they return my calls?" You start to question if the connection was real at all.

Its two weeks post conference. "That was such a waste of time!" you complain. "I am sick of calling and emailing with no response! I spent A LOT of money to attend that conference, considering hotel costs, travel, food, and time away from my business! Why do I keep investing money on these stupid conferences when I NEVER recoup my costs, much less make any profit?"

If you have had this experience, you are not alone. To avoid post-networking regret, having a conference networking strategy and follow-up system in place is critical. By setting a goal for what you want to accomplish, you'll feel more successful when you see progress. Being clear on the discipline required to follow up makes it easier to be committed to the journey instead of expecting quick results. Surprisingly, the most successful sales professionals must reach out six to twelve times to connect with their potential clients. By just using a consistent follow-up system, you will be miles ahead of your competition! Most sales professionals give up way too early!

After the first contact, 43 percent of people have given up. After the second contact, 68 percent of people have given up. After the third contact, 80 percent of people have given up. Most people never make it past the third try! Having a networking strategy helps you understand and communicate "why" you want to keep in touch. Clarity creates urgency for both parties, so staying connected becomes a priority when each person gets back into the office and catch-up work begins. Remember, don't take it personally. Just like you have a full inbox, a dozen phone calls to return, and a stack of files to review

> With a plan, a system, and some practice; you can follow up flawlessly.

waiting for you; so do the people with whom you have connected. By not returning your call immediately, they may not be saying "I am not interested." Instead, what they might be saying is "I am interested, but other things have taken priority at the moment. If you are persistent, I will

eventually schedule some time to talk with you, learn more about who you are and what you provide, and possibly invest in your product or service."

Don't give up and don't talk yourself out of your imminent success. Remember, you etch yourself on the forefront of your prospective client's mind when you creatively stay in touch and prove your value. With a plan, a system, and some practice; you can follow up flawlessly. I am going to be honest with you. Sometimes I just don't do the things I know I must do to grow my business. I've dealt with this for years. When I was doing sales for the staffing company for which I used to work for, I made it my business to organize my office, clean my inbox, and brainstorm new ideas. Anything to keep from picking up that stupid telephone and making calls. When I opened my own staffing company, I was super busy managing staff, running payroll, and working on my website. Once again, I had fooled myself into thinking that so long as I was "busy," I was being productive.

Eventually, I figured out that I was hiding. I was shrinking back from following up on hot leads, making cold calls, building a business. I had a very sobering realization (not being able to make payroll will do that!), and I finally had to step into my big girl pants and pick up the phone. I had to not only attend events, I had to go to events with a plan and refuse to stand around chatting with people with whom I was already acquainted. I had to get comfortable walking up to complete strangers and drumming up a conversation while listening for cues that identified them as my ideal client.

Your ability to network effectively has a direct impact on your income. Generally, fear is the biggest culprit for people who are hesitant to make sales calls or attend networking events.

If you are willing to exchange wealth for fear, it is time to examine what is going on behind the scenes. I believe that relationships are the catalyst for success, so I encourage you to determine which relationships you are avoiding. Is it really that initial interaction that is scary or is the relationship that you really need to work on the one you have with yourself? You will never present yourself more boldly than you believe you are. Take some time to evaluate why you are filling up your day with excuses disguised as being busy.

I previously said that I don't always do what's necessary either. When I feel this way, I do the same self-check I am advocating here. I make the necessary adjustments, then I get on the phone or get in front of some of my ideal clients. Remember, things won't change until you do. If you are sick of wondering how you are going to increase your income and grow your business, you need to shift in the way you do sales and networking to substantially improve your bottom line.

We have all had moments in which, as we walk away from an interaction, we replay what we wish we had said. Often in business scenarios we second guess our sales presentation, knowing that had we not been intimidated, we would have addressed their objections differently. In some cases, we get a once in a lifetime opportunity to pitch our company to a huge business mogul, but just like with some of the smaller opportunities, we once again, chicken out.

Consider the most important and impactful people in your life. What if they would have been afraid to offer you the life-altering experience you currently enjoy? I shudder to think how different my life would be if some of the most influential people in my life lacked the courage to approach me or say what needed to be said at the appropriate times. Some connections that come to mind are my husband, my pastor, my business coach, and my best friend. My life would be vastly different on all levels had any of these people been frozen in fear and neglected to offer me the solutions that they provided in my life.

I am reminded of the many times in which my lack of confidence and doubt in my ability to succeed nearly robbed my past and current clients of the success and transformation they are now experiencing. When we examine the ripple effect our words and actions have on those with whom we associate, the importance of confidence is clear. Our silence and apprehension (and sometimes unwillingness) to speak up is a thief that deprives others of remarkable opportunities. Confidence is an obligation. There is someone right now in your network who is looking for the solution you provide. Your fear of picking up the telephone or following up with them does both of you a disservice. You cannot afford to remain silent. Your network is waiting.

CHAPTER FOUR

"To be yourself in a world that is constantly trying to make you something else is the greatest accomplishment."
— Ralph Waldo Emerson

YOUR RELATIONSHIP PERSONA: KNOW THYSELF

Who are you really? Have you ever explored the question? What is your persona? What does the word mean? Persona is defined as a person's perceived or evident personality, as that of a well-known official, actor, or celebrity; personal image; public role.

How do others see you? How much do you have to do with their perception? More importantly, how do you see yourself? Self-confidence refers to the way we see and think about ourselves.

Your self-confidence is made up of all the experiences and interpersonal relationships you've had in your life. Everyone you've ever met has added to or taken away from how you see yourself. Think about this: You walk past someone in a grocery store who comments on how great your hair looks. Without realizing it, your smile gets bigger. You walk a little taller. The moment you pass by a mirror, you take a glance for yourself. On the other hand, you get dressed and feel pretty good about yourself. Your spouse or another close friend makes a negative comment about your attire. You say you don't care, but you find yourself checking yourself out in the mirror without nearly as much swag as in the previous example. You ultimately change your clothes before leaving the house. How can we change these scenarios so that even though you appreciate a compliment, someone giving you one isn't so powerful that you can't function without one? How can we develop such a strong self-image that someone's personal opinion doesn't negatively rock our worlds?

Author Dr. Cindy Trimm writes, "Change doesn't start with forming new habits; it starts with asking the right questions." What questions are you asking yourself? Start by pondering the following:

- What message do I want to send?

- What makes me different?

- What are my strengths, and what am I known for?

- What am I passionate about?

- Who am I in comparison to who am I called to be?

- How do I bridge this gap?

I believe these are the most important questions: Do I love AND like myself? What do I love about myself? How can I grow and become better today?

You can't expect others to feel or do for you what you are incapable or unwilling to feel or do for yourself. You will not be able to establish and nurture strong relationships with others if your relationship with yourself continuously suffers.

In some cases, we are eager for companionship because we can't stand to be alone with our own thoughts. Once we get comfortable (and respectful) with our own private thoughts and behaviors toward ourselves, we will begin to see transformation in so many other areas of our lives. Only then will we have truly healthy and stable business and personal relationships. Remember, you can't effectively connect with

> A disjointed soul will produce disjointed relationships.

someone else when you are not connected internally. A disjointed soul will produce disjointed relationships. Internal stability creates external rewards. Don't allow your "I AM" to become distorted. Examine what you are saying to yourself. What follows "I AM" in your communication shapes your life. Be intentional

about what you say, understanding that you are creating your world with your words. If you are constantly saying "I am not good at sales calls" you won't be. Not only will your sales suffer, but you won't attract new potential clients at all because your very words are repelling them. We often attract people like us or people who can sense our insecurities and have come to take advantage of us. Either way, you have more to do with the types of relationships you have than you think.

Take some time alone to determine who you really are. Who are you attracting, and who are you repelling? How can your own thoughts, self-talk, and self-image begin to influence the types of people who come into and stay in your life? I challenge you to take a day or two (more if you have the liberty in your schedule) to do some self-evaluation. If you are brutally honest with yourself and willing to do the work, you will learn something that will help you change the way you network, sell, and improve your relationships overall. Change is completely up to you.

CHAPTER FIVE

"Assumptions are the termites
of relationships." – Henry Winkler

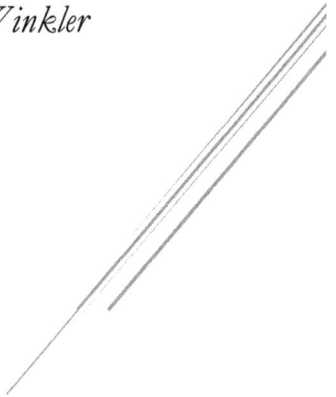

A DIFFERENT KIND OF COURTING

Almost everyone likes to feel special. Special means different things to different people, so we must take time to investigate what special means to our potential clients.

Is your potential client an extrovert or an introvert? If you think your approach can be the same across the board for all types of people, you are sadly mistaken. There are distinct differences in the way introverts and extroverts like to communicate. Let's define what we mean by these terms.

An introvert re-energizes by being alone and spends energy when in a group setting. The word introvert does not mean shy. Instead, it connotes that he or she may need alone time to recharge before he or she wants to re-enter a social setting.

An extrovert receives energy in social settings.

He or she thrives on communicating in a group setting and is often most creative when others are present to bounce ideas off of.

In some cases, an introvert needs time and quiet to gather his or her ideas and responses to a question or challenge. While an extrovert wants to process his or her thoughts with others present, often just to hear themselves talk it through.

Seldom is a person "all introvert" or "all extrovert," but there are trends that you should pay attention to:

☐   An introvert makes more and continual eye contact

☐   An introvert will appear to ponder before he or she speaks

☐   An introvert may disappear during an event, or communicate intensely with only one person

☐   An introvert may need to get to know someone before he or she opens up in a group

☐ An introvert needs to have alone time to ponder and process

☐ An extrovert is invigorated by being at a networking event interacting with people

☐ An extrovert jumps right into a conversation and thinks while he or she speaks

☐ An extrovert can be comfortable communicating with three or four people at a time

☐ An extrovert will engage many people at an event because he or she loves to meet new people

☐ An extrovert may enjoy socializing after the event

Just like dating, when networking, you must be aware of the type of person with whom you are communicating. Be cognizant of the fact that although you may like small talk, if you are dealing with an introvert, he or she may not appreciate this type of (what they might consider) meaningless interaction. Instead, be prepared to ask deeper, yet noninvasive, questions that will help you to get to know your potential client. Be willing to share more of yourself without the "sales agenda" being attached to the conversation. If you are incapable of investing

> If you think your approach can be the same across the board for all types of people, you are sadly mistaken.

in a relationship, you will struggle to develop ties with potential clients who are introverts. Sending text messages and shallow emails is not the best way to network with your introverted prospects. Picking up the phone with the intention of sincere communication is advisable if you intend follow-

up with prospective clients who are introverted.

When networking with extroverts, be aware of the social energy it may require to maintain a new relationship. When using networking as the entrance point to your sales process, you must determine your investment level. If you are an introvert, will you have the social energy to accept invitations to multiple events, should that be the case? Might it be overwhelming to accompany a potential client to lengthy meetings requiring you to be "on" the entire time?

As an introvert myself, it has taken years to develop the discipline and stamina required (for me) to network effectively in large groups. Although I don't represent all introverts in the business world, I have had countless conversations with other professionals who have a similar outlook as it pertains to the way they want to interact and how they want to be approached. I recently experienced a few scenarios that I'll share to drive the point home.

At a networking event, at which I gave the keynote speech, I was approached (or shall I say cornered) by a person who sells a piece of equipment of which I have no need. It is a medical device that I don't need or desire. Instead of asking me appropriate discovery type questions to determine if I was his ideal client, the salesperson persisted in vomiting his pitch to me at length. Although this would probably be a turn off for anyone, it was tremendously painful for me. It took every professional bone in my body to keep me from yelling "SHUT UP!!!" Eventually, I was able to make my escape and found myself avoiding him the remainder of the event. I even had another attendee come over and ask if she could just talk to me so she would appear occupied in order not to be targeted by the same guy. This may be an extreme (but true) example; however, it is important to understand how excessive and unnecessary small talk may come across to an introvert. Instead of being magnetic with your conversation, you may be repelling the person with whom you had hoped to do business.

If you are an introvert with intentions of networking with extroverts, you must first determine what you are comfortable and willing to do. Always be yourself, but understand you may have to stretch out of your comfort zone in order to develop rapport. Although it may not be your favorite thing to do, be friendly and make small talk. Practice good eye contact. Be prepared to respond faster than you normally would if asked a question. Often extroverts think by talking out loud, so allow them space to talk without interruption so they can establish a train of thought for themselves on your product or service.

CHAPTER SIX

"I don't want anyone who doesn't want me." – Oprah Winfrey

DON'T ALLOW THE FEAR
OF REJECTION TO GET YOU REJECTED

As humans, we crave relationships. Sometimes we want these relationships so badly that we don't think we can live without them. Our fear of people not feeling the same about us as we do them can cause us to behave in ways that seem desperate. Instead of causing them to run to us, we make them flee from our suffocating embrace, gasping for air with intentions to cease communication. Fear of rejection causes us to either avoid entering into new relationships altogether or to pursue new opportunities behaving as a semi-stalker, scaring off our potential new friends. When I hear clients tell me about their aversion to sales, I wonder where their hesitancies originated. Is it an inability to communicate effectively or is it a fear of hearing the word no? Is there a resurfacing of the feelings you had when an old flame said he or she

would call but did not? Are you reminded of a

time when you really liked another kid in school,

but he or she didn't even acknowledge your

presence? Whether we think about the reasons

we don't network or sell very well or not, there

is likely a deeper reason
than we may be willing
to delve into. Rejection

**Fear of rejection is the
death of all sales and
networking success.**

is just an event that only

takes a moment; then

it's over. But the fear of

rejection can become

a way of life. Fear of rejection is the death of all

sales and networking success. This fear will keep

you stuck behind your desk when you should be

out meeting new prospective clients. It will cause

you to forfeit conversations that should move

you beyond the first interaction.

The first step in firing fear from the sales process

is to stop taking things personally. Often rejection
isn't even about us, yet we put ourselves in the
center of the target and wait for the shot. If
we can reframe the situation without us at the
center, we can alleviate some of the pain that
comes along with rejection. Consider maybe
your prospect is having a bad day. Maybe he
or she sincerely doesn't have time to chat now,
or even possibly, he or she is just a jerk and isn't
your ideal client at all. Realize that everyone you
approach will not need your product or service
and you aren't a fit for everyone you meet.
With that in mind, in order to increase sales, you
must talk to people and develop balanced
professional relationships. If you are hiding from
or squeezing the life out of them, you won't ever
get to experience the prosperous, profitable life
and business that you are supposed to have.
Reject rejection.

CHAPTER SEVEN

"The royal road to a man's heart is to talk to him about the things he treasures most." – Dale Carnegie

NURTURE
AND CULTIVATION
(PICK UP THE PHONE)

The inspiration for this chapter comes from my own tendency to avoid making phone calls. I only teach this so well because I have struggled with it myself, and I know how "heavy" the telephone can be when it is time to make follow-up calls. In the past, this has been my day:

7:30 a.m.: It's too early to start calling people; I'll give it a little while

8:30 a.m.: I'd better get my desk organized so I know what I am supposed to be doing

10:00 a.m.: Time to send out some emails and cards for my list

11:00 a.m.: I should make some calls; however, folks are probably getting ready to go to lunch by now

1:00 p.m.: People are just getting back from

lunch; I'll give them a while to get settled in

2:00 p.m.: Make a few calls; no answer. Get discouraged. Go do something else.

3:00 p.m.: *Finds a hundred other things to do instead of making calls

4:00 p.m.: People are starting to wind down for the day; I don't want to bother them

5:00 p.m.: Well, it is too late to call anyone now. I'll call them tomorrow.

For me, unnecessary busyness is indicative of fear. I can easily get busy doing everything except what needs to be done to move my business forward. Don't judge me. I know that many of you have had different variations of the day I just described, and your bank account reflects it just like mine did.

Follow-up is the most important part of the networking and sales process, yet the average entrepreneur struggles with it in a huge way. A different approach might be to create follow-up time blocks of just a few calls. For instance, strive to make five connections between 9:00 a.m. and 10:00 a.m. (that's connections, not just calls). I sometimes give myself permission not to leave voicemail so I can just keep making my calls until I reach five live voices during my call blocks. You can then take the half hour between 2:00 p.m. and 2:30 p.m. and strive to reach three live voices within the call block. That is only one and a half hours out of your day, and it is broken up into manageable chunks.

> Consistent, effective activity is one of the best ways to get out of a follow-up rut.

If you are currently struggling with this, how much would your business change if you were able to make eight new connections per day? Your time will adjust for longer conversations, but if you are inviting them to schedule a more in depth conversation at a later date, it shouldn't take too long. Play with your follow-up time blocks, as your tribe may be more reachable at different times.

Consistent, effective activity is one of the best ways to get out of a follow-up rut. Don't stay stuck. Don't be afraid to pick up the telephone, begin to cultivate relationships, and see bankable results in your business.

CHAPTER EIGHT

"The greatest compliment that was ever paid me was when someone asked me what I thought and attended to my answer." – Henry David Thoreau

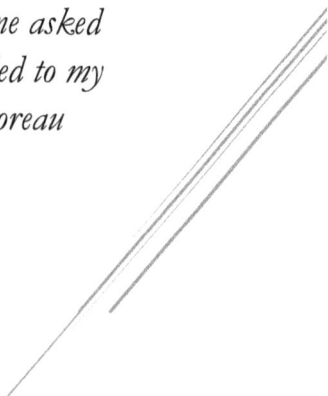

RELATIONSHIP EXPANSION

Why is it so important to cultivate relationships and treat them as lifelong friendships instead of sales transactions? When you have a nurturing approach, it changes the feel of the interaction, the way you communicate, and the care that is shown in the relationship. Yes, you can have true relationships in business, and you should if you want to develop a lasting, loyal customer base.

I love direct sales companies. I have had a successful run with a few of them. I have several clients who have blossoming direct sales businesses. I mean those who get to walk across the stage at their annual conventions and take the cruises, and win the lavish prizes. Those who get it—who really understand how to cherish client relationships.

On the other hand, I have had several people with whom I have had casual interactions over the years approach me, after no contact in years, out of the blue, call me (or worse, Facebook inbox me) to tell me how they want to reconnect or that they have something special they want to share with me.

I'm often willing to help someone if I can, so I will allow the call if I have time. I find it highly offensive, however, when I realize that the only reason he or she wanted to reconnect was to introduce me to his or her new product (not to reconnect or find

> You can have true relationships in business, and you should if you want to develop a lasting, loyal customer base.

out anything about me as a person). Yet, that is not what really gets under my skin. It's when I tell the person I am not interested, how he or she immediately disconnects and mysteriously go back into obscurity.

Just like with any other industry, direct sales professionals must nurture relationships and invest time in prospective client cultivation. Although dozens of companies teach their representatives creative and effective ways to locate and secure new customers, there are many others that just tell them they will get a new car if they sell more stuff. The latter breeds desperate, sleazy sales tactics that give the whole industry a bad name. Regardless of the product or service you sell, you can develop the type of rapport with people that makes them seek you out instead of the other way around.

I love working with direct sales teams, because I believe you can complement the "company mandated training" with techniques and strategies that cause you to stand out even among your own colleagues.

I used to sell makeup with a direct sales company, so I will use them as an example. If there are a million make up consultants in direct sales, why would I want you to be my personal consultant? Make me believe that you care about my skin care needs. Give me a reason to give you my hard-earned money instead of one of the other dozen reps who have called me with the same verbatim spiel earlier this week.

If you are in a saturated market or a company with hundreds of other reps, don't you want to stand out? The only way you can stand out at a networking event and make a memorable impact on your prospective client is to network differently. Refuse to only call everyone on your list of a hundred folks you went to school with or worked with in the past, including your dentist, your doctor, your former teachers, your butcher, etc. You get my point I am sure. In addition to making those necessary calls, also create a system to know how often to call them, what other methods of connection can you initiate, and how to determine how long to keep them on your list. Although not everyone will be a fit for your product or your team, if you approach every "no" with an "on to the next one" attitude you will miss multiple opportunities to help people and grow your business.

As sales professionals, we have to stop seeing every person as an opportunity and start seeing every person as a person who we can generously serve. In the process, we may potentially gain a long-term customer who helps us expand our business by referring others who are as excited about the chance to experience the solution we provide as he or she is.

CHAPTER NINE

"Men and women are not limited by the place of their birth, not by color of their skin, but by the size of their hope."
— *John Johnson*

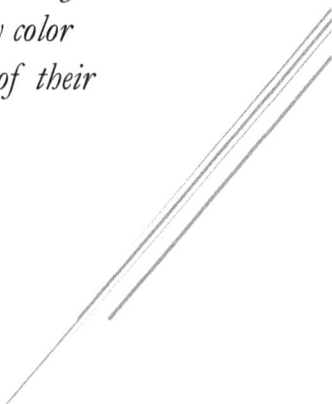

SIZE DOESN'T MATTER

Connection is why we are here. If that were not so, when God created man, Adam would have been left here alone. We are wired to develop relationships. Business becomes difficult when we try to compartmentalize our lives by thinking we can have relationships in our personal space; however, work has to be unemotional and cold.

By believing that business is only transactional, you will find yourself constantly on a hamster wheel in an effort to find new clients. Not realizing that it is much more effective to nurture the relationships you already have. These become the people who will buy their cars
 from you for decades; they make you their insurance representative for life; as their Realtor, they refer their children to you once they are old enough and ready to buy a home of their own. Generational loyalty only comes from strong

relationships.

Don't feel like you have to subject yourself to large events that make you uncomfortable if that just isn't your thing. You can easily build relationships by networking in smaller groups.

When I first started my company, I didn't have loads of money, and I didn't know exactly how to grow my business. What I did know was people. I have grown to be much more comfortable in larger groups when I speak; however, I still prefer to network for

> Generational loyalty only comes from strong relationships.

my business in smaller crowds. Because of my propensity for intimate settings, I started off by working at the local Starbucks so I could introduce myself to the person "officing" at the table next to me. People who frequented the establishment became accustomed to

seeing me there, which caused them to feel comfortable approaching me to ask me what I do for a living. This gave me an opportunity to not only share my business story, but also to hear theirs. I acquired many new clients with the approach of positioning myself in an environment conducive to networking. I often invited two to three potential clients for an impromptu networking session at my "Starbucks office," which gave me the opportunity to manage my comfort level while meeting new people.

Next, I graduated to hosting my own small sessions on a monthly basis. This gave me the ability to invite the types of people who I wanted in the room, demonstrate my expertise, and create an atmosphere that made my guests comfortable enough to learn and share about each other's business. Although I hosted my first event more than six years ago, I still have many clients from the very first meeting, I've gained dozens since then from this model, and the majority of the attendees now do business together. This was a great way to help others to dismiss the one-night stand approach and develop long-term business relationships (and friendships) that feed their bank account.

Don't be fooled into thinking that you have to use traditional networking methods or hang out at huge events to meet the right future clients.

CHAPTER TEN

"Commitment means staying loyal to what you said you were going to do long after the mood you said it in has left you." – Unknown

KEEP THE FIRE BURNING

The brilliance in long-term relationships is the effort that is invested to keep them exciting and new. Business relationships are no different. If you sell a client a product or service then cease to communicate with him or her over a long period of time, don't be surprised when he or she begins to "cheat" on you with your competitor. People will often pay attention to who is paying attention to them.

Maintaining healthy business relationships doesn't just happen. You have to develop systems to stay in touch, to add value, and to be a great partner for your clients.

For current clients, pick five clients each week to show appreciation. Send a handwritten note thanking them for their business or pick up the phone and check in with them to express your gratitude. Monthly, pick two or three clients to

have a fruit basket delivered or find out the type
of things they enjoy (such as sports, concerts,
movies) and send them tickets to an event. On
a larger scale, consider a quarterly or biannual
client appreciation event where you host clients
for a mixer or take them to an event of some sort.

The possibilities are
endless even if your
budget isn't. If doing
things on a larger
scale won't work, try
having coffee with
one or two clients
per week so you get
in front of them and

> Think of follow-up like
> a covenant. Protect
> your integrity by
> keeping your word.

stay abreast of what is going on with them and
their company. Figure out what works best for
you, but do something.

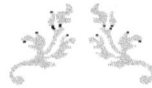

Until a prospect becomes a customer or you
determine he or she is not your ideal client after

all, you must have a follow-up routine in place. This will allow you to stay at the forefront of his or her mind so that you are the obvious choice when a need arises. Follow-up is not an email sent after an initial meeting. That's just one step in the process. You must learn to be persistent, but not stalky!

Find a way to shock and awe a prospect by sending them an above and beyond gift that adds value.

For appointment-setting success, you must reach out a number of times, using multiple media.

- Leave voicemails
- Send emails
- Drop a package in the mail
- Write a handwritten note
- Mark up an article to send
- Offer white papers or eBooks to

download from your site if it will add value for

your potential client

- Provide referrals

- Offer in-person introductions to a lead he or she needs to know

A new business relationship requires a lot of nurturing and persistence. If you think you're being a little overbearing, think again! Just ten percent of leads are made on the fourth contact—you must persist in order to connect.

Eighty percent of sales are captured between the fifth and twelfth contact with a potential customer. Developing a follow-up strategy is an important tactic. Following up with a client doesn't end at an initial phone call or email. Consistently educate your future client on the value your service adds to his or her business. Remember you are asking for a meeting not his or her first born! Just do it!

Think of follow-up like a covenant. Protect

your integrity by keeping your word. You may know what it feels like to have someone tell you he or she is interested in you and that he or she will call you, but you never hear from him or her. Once you do this in business, you immediately lose credibility. It is implied that once you ask for someone's business card you will reach out to them. Stop leaving money on the table! Keeping your commitments costs pennies, but the regret of breaking your word can cost thousands!

Don't treat your prospective clients like someone you met at some event. Treat them like the treasures they are. Don't allow fear to govern your willingness to do the work of follow-up. If so, it will also dictate the success of your business and minimize your ability to make more money and serve your tribe.

As I said earlier, relationships are the catalysts for success. You can become unstoppable in your business or career by making changes to the way you initiate and cultivate relationships. The topics addressed in this book are very near to my heart because I've either been the recipient or the giver of them.

One thing I know for sure is that, as sales professionals, we must be able to separate our own personal needs from the way we seek out new clients. When we are aggressive in our approach because we have an urgent need to make payroll or pay rent, it comes across in our delivery. Fear and desperation have an aroma. Just as you may immediately cross the street or move away from a person who has an unpleasant odor, you may inadvertently be chasing your potential clients away with an overly eager sales pitch.

If you were in a dating scenario, you would easily pick up on the motives of a person who obviously only has one thing on his or her mind. Well, the people with whom you desire to do business with also have a keen radar and can smell your intention from across the room.

If you change your approach, trust in your ability, and value yourself and your product or service, you will become a magnetic force that almost effortlessly attracts clients. I would love to hear how you've made changes and implemented systems in your networking and sales process. If you need help, I'm here.

ABOUT THE AUTHOR

Tish Times is on a mission to bring a sense of purpose and authenticity back to networking. She works with companies to amplify their business and increase profits through harnessing the power of networking, without feeling sleazy or salesy.

A corporate executive-turned-entrepreneur, Tish combines her results-driven business brain with her compassionate personal side as the owner of HireTimes Training & Coaching Group. She works with her clients one-on-one and through **in-person seminars and workshops** to develop networking strategies based on their unique personalities and tried-and-true networking and follow-up practices. She combines proven strategies with interpersonal awareness to create effective networking plans that produce results while still feeling natural. Through her signature program, **Unstoppable Confidence Networking University**, Tish helps her clients develop customized networking strategies that not only produce unparalleled results, but build genuine connections and *feel good* at the same time.

Within 2 days:
Call – If you have to leave a voicemail say
something like:

> *Hi XX, this is XX, we met at XXX…. I have a*
> *quick question for you, would you be*
> *willing to give me a quick call?*
> (People tend to call back when they feel
> like you need them for something)

Send personal email and connect on social
media

Within 2 weeks:
Schedule an in person meeting, coffee date (if
you can't do in person, use video chat - such a
Skype)
Use probing, compelling questions to understand
their business and needs

Within 2 months:
Send articles, letter updating them on your
business or industry
Call with valuable insight; determine what has
changed in their business to see if timing might
be better.

AUTOMATE THE FOLLOW UP PROCESS!

Make this easy, not overwhelming by using a robust CRM system that will give you reminders for any manual task and automatically send out any digital task!

?

What if they aren't my ideal client?

- See how you might be of assistance in other ways
- Tell them you may not be the right person to help them.
- Send them a referral of someone who can really help them

?

How do I stay in touch?

- A new business relationship requires a lot of nurturing and persistence. If you think you're being a little overbearing, think again! Just 10% of leads are made on the 4th contact - you must persist in order to connect
- Following up with a client doesn't end at an initial phone call or email, consistently educate your future client on the value your service adds to their business.

?

What should I do?

- A new business relationship requires a lot of nurturing and persistence. If you think you're being a little overbearing, think again! Just 10% of leads are made on the 4th contact - you must persist in order to connect.
- Mark up an article to send
- Offer white papers or ebooks to download from your site if it will add value for your potential client

Sample Follow up Email Sequence:

- Create an email that will be sent immediately and automatically once you enter your contact's information.
    - This email is to welcome your new prospect. It can also be used to invite them to take one more step to receive a special gift by clicking a link to confirm they want to subscribe to your electronic newsletter. Give clear instructions of what they need to do to subscribe then provide a call to action with the first email.
- When they subscribe, they should both be sent to a web page where they can access their free gift as well as receive a new email to their inbox. The new email provides access and directions using their free gift from you.
- Remind your new community member of who you are and why they are receiving your email.
- Send a feedback email within a week of receipt - Ask them what they think of your

report or product. Include another link to where they can access more complimentary goodies.

NEWTWORKING GUIDE

Dear Profitable Networker,

Networking is something we all know we SHOULD be doing and that if done correctly, it has the potential to bring forth massive rewards. I will share with you that networking definitely hasn't always been a strength of mine – I've had my share of blunders. One of those blunders was networking without a clear plan.

My experiences have made me realize I need to be crystal clear about

⬜ the events that I attend,

⬜ what I will say to the connections that I make, and

⬜ how I will keep the conversation going after the event.

If I ever miss an opportunity, I don't ever want it to be because I didn't have a clear networking plan.

Take some time to complete each section before your next networking event. You will start attending events and making great connections.

To your networking success!

YOUR NETWORKING PERSONA

Persona: person's perceived or evident personality, as that of a well-known official, actor, or celebrity; personal image; public role.

How do others see you?

_____
_____
_____
_____

How much do you have to do with their perception?

_____
_____
_____
_____

What message do you want to send?

_____

_____

_____

_____

What makes you different?

_____

_____

_____

_____

What are my strengths and what am I already known for?

_____

_____

_____

_____

What am I passionate about?

_____

_____

_____

_____

YOUR NETWORKING PERSONA

Which one are you?

(NOTE: you can have qualities from more than one persona)

Anti-Socialite

- ✓ Comfortable being alone
- ✓ Very reflective
- ✓ Being in social settings is draining
- ✓ Refuel by being alone
- ✓ Refuel by being with those who they are comfortable with
- ✓ Follow up doesn't happen
- ✓ Follow up is infrequent or shallow

Conversator

- ✓ Very confident
- ✓ Gets energy from being in social settings
- ✓ Talkative and outgoing
- ✓ Go to every event
- ✓ Networking = party
- ✓ You love getting together

Sucker

- ✓ Collect business cards
- ✓ May come across salesy
- ✓ Dominates the conversation
- ✓ The conversation is all about them

Profitable Networker

- ✓ Have a giving attitude
- ✓ About making connections
- ✓ Great listener
- ✓ Prepared for the networking event
- ✓ Asks what can I contribute
- ✓ You are systematic and sincere about their networking approach
- ✓ You are able to connect relationships with your bottom line.

Your Qualities:

_____

_____

_____

_____

_____

_____

_____

_____

Your Follow up Routine

How will you stay in contact with the connections you make?

- Make a phone call by [HOW MANY DAYS]
- Send an email in [NUMBER OF DAYS]
- Send them a "gift" (article that relates to them, a connection, something that was helpful to you, etc.)

Sample Phone Call scripts or Emails

Hey [NAME],

It was great to meet you. Thank you for you spending a few moments with me. I would love to get to know you better.

Or

Hey [NAME],

Just wanted to reach out to you after meeting you at [EVENT].

I would love to learn more about your company and help you grow your business. Let's sit down and talk.

(This allows me to continue to stay in touch with them on a weekly basis.)

Write your follow up email

_____
_____
_____
_____
_____
_____
_____
_____

Write your follow up script

_____
_____
_____
_____
_____
_____
_____
_____

Sample follow up tracker

Name	Company	Email	Phone	2 day	2 wks	2 mos